# Strawberry Pie

Jamie Norton
Illustrated by Margaret Power

Grandma drove us to the strawberry farm.
"We need the best strawberries for my pie!" she said.

"Look at the white flowers!" I said.

"Don't pick the flowers," said Grandma.
"Those flowers will grow into strawberries!"

"Look at the little green strawberries," I said.

"Don't pick the green ones," said Grandma.
"They are not ripe yet."

"Look at those big red strawberries," I said.
"They are under the leaves."

"Let's pick them!" said Grandma.

We filled the basket with strawberries.
We ate some, too!

"Let's go home to make strawberry pie!" said Grandma.

Strawberries this way →

We helped Grandma make the pie.

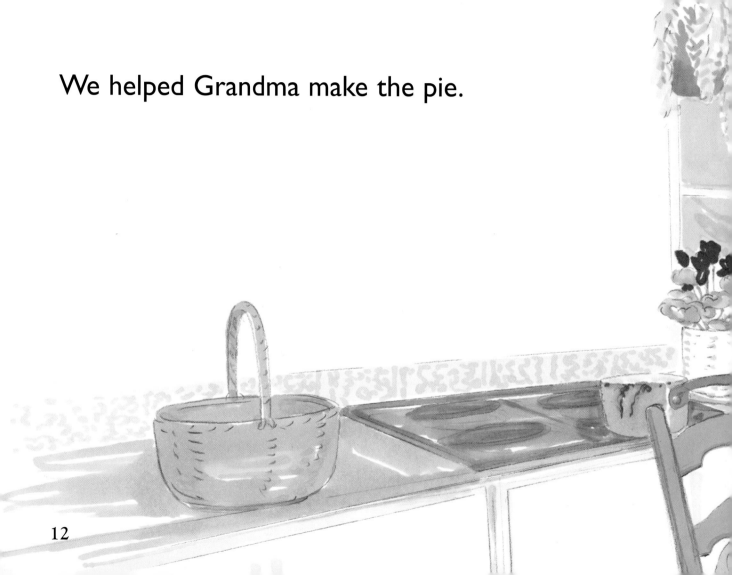

We helped Grandma eat the pie, too.

"This is the best strawberry pie ever!" I said.

"And I have a surprise for you," said Grandma.

"A strawberry plant!" I said.

"Now you can grow your own strawberries,"
said Grandma.